Nigerian Political Registry

Nigerian Political Registry
1944 - 2016

Printed by Create Space: a Division of Amazon Company

Preface

Early Nigerian political activists maybe shocked their names are not among leading Nigerian political gladiators of the nineteenth and twentieth century, but their contributions are no less important than those who enthroned Nigeria independence or played roles in the continuing gimmicks called Nigerian politics.

Among leading political actors at various stages of the struggle are Sapara Williams, Adeniyi Jones, H.O. Davies, Samuel Akinsanya, Jibowu, Solanke, Adeyemo Alakija, Mrs. Funmilayo Ramsome-kuti, Mrs. Margaret Ekpo, Harold Dappa-biriye, Kenekueyero B. Omoteseye, Louis Phillippe Ojukwu, Mbonu Ojike, Earnest Okoli, Eyo Ita, A.C. Nwapa, Eni Njoku, Okio Arikpo, M.C.K. Ajuluckukwu, Abiodun Aloba, Nduka Eze, G. Onyeagbula, M. Aina, G. Ebo, J. Inoma, S. Aderibigbe, Jereton Mariere, Gawain Westray Bell, Solomon Muna, N.N. Mbile, R.N. Charley, V.T. Lainjo, John Ngu Foncha, S. A. George, M.N. Forju, A.T. Ngala, J.T. Ndze, J.C. Kangsen, Sarna Ndi, P.M. Motomby-Woleta, Kashim Ibrahim, Adesoji Aderemi, Joseph Fadahunsi, Raji Abdallah, Adesanya Idowu, Osita Agwuna, Anthony Enahoro, Mokwugo Okoye, Kalu Ezera, Oged Macaulay, Smart Ebbi, etc.

Patrick Nwakamma Ottih (1918 – November 18, 2004) was a leading African nationalist allied to the Casablanca Group bloc of the African Nationalist Movement when aspiration for Nigeria independence was limited to the Lagos territory, and her political warriors were mainly members of the Lagos Youth Movement, but with Dr. Nnamdi Azikiwe's ferocious nationalism and Nigerian political gladiators like Herbert Macaulay colligating around him; Chief Ottih, though a member of the radical wing of the African Nationalist Movement saw the need to tone down his rhetoric's and associate with the Lagos group. He was a foundation member of the National Council of Nigeria and the Cameroon's in 1944, when Southern Cameroon was part of Nigeria.

With Southern Cameroon agitation for a separate political entity from Nigeria, he joined forces with political groups closer to his business interest, and allied with Kamerun National Congress and later Kamerun Peoples Party (political groups closely allied to Nigeria). Although both parties merged and became Cameroon Peoples National Convention, he retained membership in the National Council of Nigeria and the Cameroon's, later called National Convention of Nigerian Citizens, and participated in the affairs of both countries. In 1959, he was enlisted by his local community interest group called Oguta County Council Leaders of Thought to contest for Nigeria House of Representatives, but he declined the offer. He remained affiliated to the two political groups and made contributions to the socioeconomic and political developments of both countries.

During the Nigeria-Biafra war, he accepted entreaties from Biafran delegations and financed Biafran diplomatic activities; converted the Cameroon branch of Igbo State Union to the Biafran Movement and organized relief aids for Biafran refugees. At the collapse of the Biafran republic, he returned to Southeastern Nigeria and was appointed a councilor.

Emmanuel Mbela Lifafa Endeley (1916-1988) was a Southern Cameroon politician who served as Nigeria labor minister during British colonial era and was familiar with Nigeria political landscape than his counterparts in Southern Cameroon. A medical doctor of wealthy heritage, his Bakweri native was a tiny population in Southern Cameroon, and that factor more than anything else was responsible for his failure to determine their political destiny.

Whereas he was successful in stirring the political leadership of Southern Cameroon as a member of Eastern Nigeria House of Assembly at Enugu, and Nigeria legislative council at Lagos, and as Prime Minister of colonial Southern Cameroon, he later lost to a political novelty. And although he secured a regional autonomy and established a House of Assembly for Southern Cameroon, he compromised his political principle and leaped into ethnic chauvinism like (John Ngu Foncha) his chief political opponent.

However, he later realized his political blunder and attempted to renew alliance with Nigeria, but it was too late. His vacillation on a key policy issue had shifted public opinion and seriously damaged his political standing. Nevertheless, his shift of policy position preserved his honor among Southern Cameroon people.

Herbert Samuel Heelas Macaulay (Nov. 14, 1864- May 7, 1946) was a famous African nationalist who pioneered early Nigeria political struggles, and founded the Lagos Youth Movement, which became Nigeria Youth Movement, and Nigeria National Democratic Party. He also co-founded the National Council of Nigeria and the Cameroon's alongside Dr. Nnamdi Azikiwe, and served as its first President.

Benjamin Nnamdi Azikiwe (November 16, 1904 – May 11, 1996) was a journalist and publisher of the West Africa pilot newspaper, through which he criticized British colonial administrations. He joined early Nigeria nationalists and became a member of Nigeria National Democratic Party, and co-founded the National Council of Nigeria and the Cameroon's alongside Herbert Macaulay. He became president of the party after the death of Herbert Macaulay. His legislative experience started when he won a seat to Nigeria Legislative Council in Lagos (1947–51), and Western Nigeria House of Assembly (1952-53). He was leader of opposition in Western Nigeria House of Assembly before relocating to Eastern Nigeria where he became Premier. He was President of the Nigeria senate before he became Governor General of Nigeria, and later President of Nigeria.

Abubakar Tafawa Balewa (December 1912- January 15, 1966) was a leading Northern Nigeria politician and member of Nigeria Legislative Council in Lagos. He was elected to Northern Nigeria House of Assembly and Nigeria House of Representatives prior to becoming Prime Minister.

Ahmadu Belo (June 12, 1910-January 15, 1966) was the only Premier of Northern Nigeria. He held the traditional title of Sardauna of Sokoto and was the leader of Northern People's Congress that governed the country until his untimely death on January 15, 1966.

Obafemi Awolowo (March 9, 1909 – May 9, 1987) was Premier of Western Nigeria and leader of Action Group and Unity Party of Nigeria. He was also leader of opposition in Nigeria House of Representatives in the first republic. During Yakubu Gowon's military administration, he served as Vice Chairman of Nigeria executive council and minister of finance.

Michael Iheonukara Okpara (December 1920 – December 17, 1984) was a medical doctor prior to entering politics. During Nnamdi Azikiwe's premiership in Eastern Nigeria, he served as minister of health, agriculture, and production before he became Premier. He later served as political advisor to the Biafran government during the Nigeria-Biafra war.

Samuel Akintola (July 6, 1910 – January 15, 1966) was deputy leader of Action Group and leader of opposition in Nigeria House of Representatives. He served as minister of health, communication, and aviation in Abubakar Tafawa Balewa administration prior to becoming Premier of Western Nigeria.

Dennis Chukwudi Osadebay (June 29, 1911 – December 26, 1994) was legal advisor to the National Council of Nigeria and the Cameroon's. He was leader of opposition in Western Nigeria House of Assembly before he became President of the Nigeria senate. His last political position was Premier of Mid-West Nigeria.

Abyssinia Akweke Nwafor Arize (1915 – 1999) was a member of Eastern Nigeria House of Chiefs. He held other positions after joining politics including serving as a member of Eastern Nigeria House of Assembly, President of the Nigeria senate, and acting President of Nigeria.

Festus Okotie-Eboh (1912-1966) was finance minister in Abubakar Tafawa Balewa administration, and a leading member of the National Convention of Nigerian Citizens.

Kingsley Ozuomba Mbadiwe (1915 – 1990) was the tenacious politician commonly known as KO or Man of Timber and Caliber.
He was a member of the House of Representatives and Eastern Nigeria House of Assembly. He also served as minister of lands and natural resources, communications, aviation, trade, and personal advisor to President Shehu Shagari on national assembly affairs.

Jaja Anucha Ndubuisi Wachukwu (Jan. 1918 – Nov. 7, 1996) was the first speaker of the House of Representatives. He also served as ambassador to the United Nations, foreign minister, and a senator.

Alvan Ezenwa Ikoku (1900-1971) was President of Nigerian Union of Teachers; a member of Eastern Nigeria legislature and Nigeria Legislative Council. He was also President of United National Party and leader of opposition in Eastern Nigeria House of Assembly. During the Nigeria- Biafra war, he served as Chairman of Biafran Constituent Assembly.

Akanu Ibiam (November 29, 1906-1995) was a missionary doctor of the Church of Scotland Mission. He was a councilor at Afikpo Divisional Council and member of Eastern Nigeria House of Assembly before he became Governor of Eastern Nigeria. He also served as advisor to the government of Biafra during the Nigeria-Biafra war.

Louis Nwachukwu Mbanefo (May 13, 1911–1977) was a member of Eastern Nigeria House of Assembly and Chief Justice of Eastern Nigeria. He also served as a justice of the Nigeria Supreme Court, and a judge at the International court of justice. He was also Chief Justice of the Republic of Biafra.

Taslim Olawale Elias (November 11, 1914- August 14, 1991) was Attorney General and Chief Justice of Nigeria, and President of the International court of justice.

Joseph Sarwuan Tarka (July 10, 1932 – March 30, 1980) was minister of transport and communication in Yakubu Gowon's military administration. He earlier served as leader of United Middle Belt Congress.

Mallam Aminu Kano (1920 - April 17, 1983) was a liberal politician and a powerful force in Nigeria politics. He led Northern Elements Progressive Union in the first republic and Peoples Redemption Party in the second republic. He also served as commissioner for communication in Yakubu Gowon's military administration.

Kenneth Onwuka Dike (1917 – 1983) was Vice Chancellor of University of Ibadan and Chairman of the Association of Commonwealth Universities. He also served as Chairman of Nigeria National Archives and roving ambassador for the Biafran government.

Chike Edozien Umuezei Obi (April 7, 1921- March 13, 2008) was a member of the House of Representatives in the first republic. He was also a member of Eastern Nigeria House of Assembly and general secretary of the Dynamic party.

Albert Chinualumogu Achebe (November 16, 1930 – March 21, 2013) was author of Things fall Apart (1958), No Longer at Ease (1960), Arrow of God (1964), A Man of the People (1966), Anthills of the Savannah (1987), etc. He served as Chairman of Biafran National Guidance Committee, and deputy national Vice President of Peoples Redemption Party.

Wole Soyinka was born on July 13, 1934. He is a playwright and noble prize winner in literature. He played an enormous role in attempting to prevent the Nigeria-Biafra war and was imprisoned for his efforts. He served as Chairman of Nigeria Federal Road Safety Commission.

Christian Chukwuma Onoh (April 27, 1927 – May 5, 2009) was a member of the House of Representatives in the first republic and later served as Chairman of Nigeria Coal Corporation and Nigeria Mining Corporation, and Associated Ore Mines. He also served as Governor of Anambra State.

Tai Solarin (August 20, 1922 – June 27, 1994) was the proprietor of the Mayflower school. He also founded Mayflower junior high school and sponsored over 300 hundred students in Nigeria and abroad and at various levels of education. He served Nigeria in several forms and in government.

Other first republic political leaders include Raymond Njoku, Muhammadu Ribadu, Aja Wachukwu, J.M. Johnson, Kolawole Balogun, Mathew Mbu, Adegoke Adelabu, Inuwa Wada, Ayo Rosiji, Zanna Bukar Dipcharima, Maitama Sule, Olu Akinfosile, Usman Sarki, T.O.S Benson, Risa Yar'Adua, Augustus Akinloye, Adeniran Ogunsanya, Adeleke Adedoyin, Richard Akinjide, Adade Lamuye, Moses Majekodunmi, Jacob Obande, Mbazulike Amaechi, F.R.A. Williams, etc.

Shehu Usman Aliyu Shagari was born on February 25, 1925, and served as President of Nigeria in the second republic. He was a member of Nigeria House of Representatives in the first republic, and served as commissioner for economic development, habitation and reconstruction, and finance in Yakubu Gowon's military administration.

Waziri Kolo Ibrahim (February 26, 1926- 1992) was a prominent political figure and presidential nominee of Great Nigeria Peoples Party in the second republic. He served as minister of economic development and health in Abubakar Tafawa Balewa administration.

Alexander Ifeanyichukwu Ekwueme was born on October 21, 1932, and served as Vice President of Nigeria 1979-83 and leader of G34 political group that culminated to Peoples Democratic Party. He was Chairman of the board of trustees of Nigeria Institute of Architects.

Joseph Wayas was born on May 21, 194, and served as President of the Nigeria senate on the platform of National Party of Nigeria. He also served as South Eastern State commissioner for transport.

Abubakar Olusola Saraki (May 17, 1033 – November 14, 2012) was majority leader in the senate during Shehu Shagari administration, and a leading member of the National Party of Nigeria.

Solomon Lar (April 1933 – October 9, 2013) was a member of the House of Representatives and parliamentary secretary in Abubakar Tafawa Balewa administration. He later served as Governor of Plateau State 1979 -83, and Chairman of Peoples Democratic Party.

Samuel Onunaka Mbakwe (1929 – January 5, 2004) was a prominent lawyer in Port Hardcourt City, Rivers State, before the Nigeria-Biafra war. He became famous for his struggle against seizures of properties of Igbo speaking people in Rivers State, Nigeria. He later became Governor of Imo State 1979-83.

Lateef Kayode Jakande was born on Jul y 23, 1929, and served as Governor of Lagos State 1979-83. He was a journalist and editor of Tribune newspapers prior to establishing Lagos news, and served as President of newspaper proprietors association of Nigeria.

James Ajibola Idowu Ige (September 13, 1930 – December 23, 2001) was a member of Action Group and Unity party of Nigeria. He served as Governor of Oyo State 1979 -83 before joining Olusegun Obasanjo administration as minister of mines and power, and later attorney general and minister for Justice. He was assassinated while serving as attorney general and minister for Justice.

Oloye Victor Olabisi Onabanjo (1927 – April 14, 1990) was Chairman of Ijebu Ode local government council before his election as Ogun State Governor 1979-83, on the platform of Unity Party of Nigeria.

Michael Adekunle Ajasin (November 28, 1908 – October 3, 1979) was national Vice President of Action Group and member of the House of Representative. He was elected Governor of Ondo State 1979 – 83, on the platform of Unity Party of Nigeria.

Ambrose Folorunsho Alli (September 22, 1929 – September 22, 1989) was a medical doctor and lecturer at University of Ibadan and Ahmadu Belo University, prior to becoming Bendel State Governor 1979-83.

Clement Nyong Isong (April20, 1920 – May 29, 2000) was Governor of Central Bank of Nigeria during Yakubu Gowon's military administration, and later served as Governor of Cross River State 1979-83.

Melford Obiene Okilo (November 30, 1933 – July 5, 2008) was a member of the House of Representatives and parliamentary secretary, and minister in Abubakar Tafawa Balewa administration. He became Governor of River State 1979-83, and later served as a senator.

James Ifeanyichukwu Nwobodo was born on May 10, 1940, and served as Governor of Anambra State 1979 – 83. He was Chairman of Enugu Rangers International Football Club and chair of Anambra State branch of Nigeria Peoples Party. He later served as a senator.

Muhammadu Abubakar Rimi (1940 – April 4, 2010) was deputy national secretary of Peoples Redemption Party prior to becoming Governor of Kano State 1979-83. He later served as a senator.

Abdulkadir Balaraba Musa was born on August 21, 1936. He is a liberal politician and leading member of Peoples Redemption Party. He became Governor of Kaduna State in 1979, but was impeached in 1981. He remains active in Nigeria politics and has served in several other capacities.

Aper Aku (1938 – 1988) was Chairman of Kwande local government council prior to becoming Governor of Benue State 1979 -83, on the platform of National Party of Nigeria. He is still held highly as a visionary leader and the best governor that ever ruled the state.

Adamu Atta (October 18, 1927 – May 1, 2014) was permanent secretary in the federal ministry of finance prior to entering politics. He was Governor of Kwara State 1979-83, on the platform of National Party of Nigeria.

Mohammed Goni was born in 1942, and served as Governor of Borno State 1979 – 83, on the platform of Great Nigeria Peoples Party. He was a civil servant prior to heading Nigeria National Supply Company.

Abubakar Tatari Ali (1929 – May 28, 1993) was commissioner for education prior to becoming Governor of Bauchi State 1979-83, on the platform of National Party of Nigeria. He is accredited with laying infrastructural foundation for modern Bauchi State.

Abba Musa Rimi was born in 1940 and served as Governor of Kaduna State from June 1981 to October 1983, on the platform of Peoples Redemption Party. His party was in the minority in the state assembly.

Abubakar barde (1938 – June 17, 2002) served as Governor of Gongola State 1979-83, but resigned due to conflicts with the state assembly. He ran again in 1983 on the platform of Nigeria Peoples Party, but lost.

Mohammed Awwal Ibrahim was Governor of Niger State 1979-83, on the platform of National Party of Nigeria. He became Emir of Suleja in 1993 but was deposed in 1994. He was restored in 2000, and made Chairman of Niger State Committee on Reformation of Almajirci.

Other second republic political leaders include Tunde Brathwaite, Richard Akinyede, R.B.K. Okafor, B.U. Nzeribe, Nwakamma Okoro, Obi Wali, Abdu Dawakin Tofa, H.P.O Udom, Sabo Bakin Zuwo, Francis Ellah, Victor Masi, etc.

Rufus Ada George was born on July 11, 1940, and served as Governor of Rivers State from January 1992-November 1993, on the platform of National Republican Convention. He later joined All Nigerian Peoples Party.

Ogbonnaya Onu was born on December 1, 1951, and served as Governor of Abia State 1992-93, on the platform of Social Democratic Party. He was Chairman of All Nigerian Peoples Party, and currently serves as minister of science and technology.

Abubakar Audu (October 24, 1947 – November 22, 2015) was Governor of Kogi State 1992- 93, on the platform of National Republican Convention and again1999-2003, under All Nigerian Peoples Party. He ran again in 2015, but died of heart attack before he was declared the winner.

Olusegun Osoba was born on July 15, 1939, and served as Governor of Ogun State 1992 – 93, on the platform of Social Democratic Party, and again from 1999 –2003, under Alliance for Democracy.

Bukar Abba Ibrahim was born in October 1950, and served as Governor of Yobe State 1992 - 93, on the platform of Social Democratic Party and again 1999 – 2007, under All Nigerian Peoples Party.

Okwesilieze Nwodo was born on July 28, 1950, and served as Governor of Enugu State 1992 – 93, on the platform of Social Democratic Party. He later became Chairman of Peoples Democratic Party.

Jolly Tavoro Nyame was born on December 25, 1955, and served as Governor of Taraba State 1992 - 93, on the platform National Republican Convention, and again 1999 - 2007, under Peoples Democratic Party.

John Odigie Oyegun was born August 12, 1939, and served as governor of Edo State from 1992-93, on the platform of Social Democratic Party. He currently serves as Chairman of All Progressives Congress.

Chukwuemeka Ezeife was born on November 20, 1939, and served as Governor of Anambra State 1992-93, on the platform of Social Democratic Party. He's been active in Nigeria political affairs.

Kabiru Ibrahim Gaya was born on June 16, 1952 and served as Governor of Kano State 1992 – 93, on the platform of National Republican Convention. He later served in the senate under All Nigerian Peoples Party.

Mohammed Shaaba Lafiagi was Governor of Kwara State from January 1992-November 1993, on the platform of Social Democratic Party. He later served in the senate under Peoples Democratic Party.

Rev. Father Moses Orshio Adasu (June 12, 1945 – November 20, 2005) was Governor of Benue State from January 1992- November 1993, on the platform of Social Democratic Party.

Olusegun Mathew Okikiola Aremu Obasanjo was born march 5, 1937, and served as President of Nigeria 1999 – 2007. He also served as military head of state 1976 – 79, and was chief of staff supreme headquarters. His presidency was tainted with numerous politically instigated assassinations.

Atiku Abubakar was born November 25, 1946, and served as Nigeria Vice President 1999-2007. He contested for president in 2007 on the platform of Action Congress of Nigeria, and was deputy director of Nigeria custom service.

Evans Enwerem (October 29, 1935 – August 2, 2007) was President of the Nigeria senate, and Governor of Imo State from January 1992- November 93. He was a businessman prior to entering politics.

Chuba Wilberforce Okadigbo (December 17, 1941 – September 25, 2003) was a prominent politician and President of the Nigeria senate. He also served as political advisor to President Shehu Shagari in the second republic. He was a lecturer at University of Nigeria, Nsukka, prior to entering politics.

Anyim Pius Anyim was born on February 19, 1961, and served as President of the Nigeria senate, on the platform of Peoples Democratic Party. He also served as secretary to the government under President Goodluck Jonathan.

Adolphus Ndaneweh Wabar was born in 1948, and served as President of the Nigeria senate, on the platform of Peoples Democratic Party. He was removed from office due to corruption, but continued to serve through the end of his term.

Kenneth Ugwu Nnamani was born on November 2, 1942, and elected to the senate on the platform of Peoples Democratic Party. He became President of the Nigeria senate, and thwarted the third term ambition of President Olusegun Obasanjo, during a difficult time in the history of the country.

Ibrahim Mantu was a senator from Plateau State and a colorful politician in Nigeria third republic. He served as Deputy President of the Nigeria senate and Chairman of Nigeria constitution review committee.

Dorothy Nkem Akunyili (July 14, 1954 – June 7, 2014) was Director General of National Agency for Food and Drug Administration and Control (NAFDAC) and of remarkable service in Nigerian society. She later served as minister for information and communication in Goodluck Jonathan administration.

Ngozi Okonjo-Iweala was born on June 13, 1954, and served as finance minister in Olusegun Obasanjo and Goodluck Jonathan administrations, and briefly as foreign minister. She also served as Vice President at the World Bank.

Bola Ahmed Tinubu was born March 29, 1952, and served as Governor of Lagos State from May 29, 1999 – May 29 2007, on the platform of Alliance for democracy. He became a prominent political figure as leader of Action Congress of Nigeria, and serves as national leader of All Progressives Congress.

Peter Otunuya Odili was born on August 15, 1948, and served as Governor of Rivers State 1999 - 2007, on the platform of Peoples Democratic Party. He almost became his party's presidential nominee in 2007.

Donald Duke was born September 30, 1961, and served as Governor of Cross Rivers State 1999 – 2007, on the platform of Peoples Democratic Party. He was credited with transforming the state and promoting tourism.

Orji Uzor Kalu was born April 21, 1960, and served as Governor of Abia State from May 1999 – May 2007, on the platform of Peoples Democratic Party. He was a successful businessman prior to entering politics, but his administration was tainted with mysterious deaths.

Obong Victor Bassey Attah was born on November 20, 1938, and served as Governor of Akwa Ibom State from May 1999 – May 2007, on the platform of Peoples Democratic Party. He was Chairman of the governor's forum.

Mohammed Rabi'u Musa Kwankwaso was born on October 2, 1956, and served as Governor of Kano State 1999 – 2003, on the platform of Peoples Democratic Party. He lost his re-election bid, but became governor again 2011-2015, on the same platform, and was a presidential candidate in 2015.

Achike Udenwa was born in 1948, and served as Governor of Imo State 1999 -2007, on the platform of Peoples Democratic Party. He later served as minister of commerce and industry in Umaru Musa Yar'Adua administration, but the murder of Mr. Uche Ogbe, a lecturer at Alvan Ikoku College of Education tainted his tenure.

Samuel Ominyi Egwu was born in June 20, 1954, and served as Governor of Ebonyi State 1999 – 2007, on the platform of Peoples Democratic Party. He later served as minister of education in Umaru Musa Yar'Adua administration.

Abdukareem Adebisi Bamidele Akande was born on January 16, 1939, and served as Governor of Osun State 1999 – 2003, on the platform of Alliance for Democracy. He was Chairman of Action Congress of Nigeria, and All Progressives Congress.

George Akume was born December 27, 1953, and served as Governor of Benue State 1999 - 2007, on the platform of Peoples Democratic Party. He later served as minority leader in the senate from 2011 – 2015, on the platform of Action Congress of Nigeria.

Ibrahim Shekarau was born November 5, 1955, and served as Governor of Kano State 2003 – 2011, on the platform of All Nigerian Peoples Party. He was a presidential candidate in 2011, and later served as minister for education.

Mohammed Alabi Lawal (1946 – November 15, 2006) was Governor of Kwara state 1999 - 2003 on the platform of Peoples Democratic Party, but lost his reelection bid. He previously served as military Governor of Ogun State during Ibrahim Babangida's military administration.

Diepreye Solomon Peter Alamieyeseigha (November 16, 1952 – October 10, 2015) was Governor of Bayelsa State 1999 – 2005, on the platform of Peoples Democratic Party. He was impeached and removed from power, but was pardoned by his former deputy, Goodluck Jonathan, when he became president.

James Onanefe Ibori was born on August 4, 1959, and served as Governor of Delta State 1999 – 2007, on the platform of Peoples Democratic Party. He was found guilty of money laundering and currently in prison.

Ahmadu Adamu Mu'azu was born June 11, 1955, and served as Governor of Bauchi State from 1999 – 2007, on the platform of Peoples Democratic Party. He later served as Chairman of the national working committee of his party.

Boni Haruna was born June 12, 1957, and served as Governor of Adamawa State 1999 – 2007, on the platform of Peoples Democratic Party. He defected to All Progressives Congress, and currently serves as minister for youth development in Muhammadu Buhari administration.

Abubakar Habu Hashidu was born April 10, 1944, and served as Governor of Gombe State 1999 – 2003, on the platform of All Nigerian Peoples Party. He also served as commissioner for water resources, rural development, and agriculture in Ibrahim Babanjida's military administration.

Mala Kachalla (November 1941 – April 182007) was Governor of Borno State 1999 – 2003, on the platform of All Nigerian Peoples Party. He lost his re-election primary and switched to Alliance for Democracy and was defeated in the election.

Chinwoke Mbadinuju was born June14, 1945, and served as Governor of Anambra State 1999 - 2003, on the platform of Peoples Democratic Party, but failed to regain nomination. His tenure was unproductive and acrimonious, resulting to the deaths of Barrister Barnabas Igwe and his wife.

Lucky Nosakhare Igbinedion was born May 13, 1957, and served as Governor of Edo State 1999 - 2007, on the platform of Peoples Democratic Party. He previously served as Chairman of Oredo local government council.

Niyi Adebayo was born in 1958, and served as Governor of Ekiti State 1999 – 2003, on the platform of Alliance for Democracy. He was defeated in his reelection bid by the candidate of Peoples Democratic Party.

Chimaroke Nnamani was born May 1960, and served as Governor of Enugu State 1999 – 2007, on the platform of Peoples Democratic Party. His tenure was acrimonious and led to the deaths of many including Professor Chimere Ikoku.

Ibrahim Saminu Turaki was born July 14, 1963, and served as Governor of Jigawa State 1999 - 2007, on the platform of All Nigerian Peoples Party. He was accredited with decentralizing the state.

Ahmed Mohammed Makarfi was born August 8, 1956, and served as Governor of Kaduna State 1999 – 2007, on the platform of Peoples Democratic Party. He also served in the senate, and currently the acting Chairman of the national working committee of his party.

Chris Nwabueze Ngige was born on August 8, 1952, and served as Governor of Anambra State 1999- 2002, on the platform of Peoples Democratic Party. His election was overturned after three years in office, but was elected to the senate, and serves as minister of labor and employment.

Muhammad Adamu Aliero was born on January 1, 1957, and served as Governor of Kebbi State 1999 - 2007 on the platform of Peoples Democratic Party. He later served in the senate.

Abdullahi Adamu was born on July 23, 1946, and served as Governor of Nasarawa State 1999 -2007 on the platform of All Nigerian Peoples Party. He worked with Electric Corporation of Nigeria prior to entering politics.

Abdulkadir Kure served as Governor of Niger State 1999 – 2003, on the platform of All Nigerian Peoples Party, and won reelection on the platform of Peoples Democratic Party. He became the first governor to introduce sharia law in the north central zone.

Adebayo Adefarati (February 14, 1931 – March 29, 2007) served as Governor of Ondo State 1999 – 2003 on the platform of Alliance for Democracy. He also served as state commissioner for works and transport.

Lamidi Ona-Olapo Adesina (January 20, 1939 – November 11, 2012) served as Governor of Oyo State 1999 – 2003, on the platform of Alliance for Democracy. He was a leading member of Action Congress of Nigeria in later years.

Joshua Chibi Dariye was born on July 27, 1957, and served as Governor of Plateau State 1999 - 2005, on the platform of Peoples Democratic Party before he was impeached. He later won a seat in the senate on the platform of Labour Party.

Attahiru Bafarawa was born on October 4, 1954, and served as Governor of Sokoto State 1999 – 2007, on the platform of All Nigerian Peoples Party. He was a presidential candidate in 2007.

Ahmad Rufai Sani Yerima was born in July 1960, and served as Governor of Zamfara State 1999 -2007 on the platform of All Nigerian Peoples Party. He now serves as deputy minority leader in the senate.

Peter Obi was born July 19, 1961, and served as Governor of Anambra State from 2006, on the platform of All Progressive Grand Alliance, although he was temporarily removed from office but returned to complete his term and was reelected.

Ayo Fayose was born November 15, 1960, and served as Governor of Ekiti State from May 2003, on the platform of Peoples Democratic Party, but was impeached in October 2006. He won again in May 2015 on the same platform.

Olusegun Kokumo Agagu (February 16, 1948 – September 13, 2013) was Governor of Ondo State from May 2003 - February 2009 on the platform of Peoples Democratic Party, before his election was nullified.

Gbenga Daniel was born April 6, 1956, and served as Governor of Ogun State 2003- 2011 on the platform of Peoples Democratic Party. His administration was occasionally rancorous.

Olagunsoye Oyinlola was born February 3, 1951, and served as Governor of Osun State 2003 - 2010, on the platform of Peoples Democratic Party until his election was nullified.

Rashidi Adewolu Ladoja was born September 25, 1944, and served as Governor of Oyo State 2003 – 2007, on the platform of Peoples Democratic Party. He was removed from office in January 2006 but reinstated in December 2006. He was later charged for corruption after leaving office.

Christopher Alao-Akala was born June 3, 1950, and served as Governor of Oyo State 2007 - 2011, on the platform of Peoples Democratic Party. His tenure was a tumorous time in the state.

Timipre Sylva was born on July 7, 1964, and served as Governor of Bayelsa State from May 2007. He was removed from office, but returned and won reelection. However, his reelection was nullified on January 27, 2012.

Other third republic political leaders include Chukwuemeka Odumegwu Ojukwu, Francis Arthur Nzeribe, Harry Marshal, Amoinosari Dokubo, Vincent Ogbulafor, Daniel Nwanyanwu, Amadu Ali, Barnabas Gemade, George Moghalu, Victor Umah, Anthony Momoh, Mohammad Lawal Malado, Audu Ogbeh, Bello Haliru Mohammed, Bamanga Tukur, etc.

Umaru Musa Yar'Adua (August 16, 1961 – May 5, 2010) was President of Nigeria on the platform of Peoples Democratic Party. He also served as Governor of Katsina State 1999 – 2007.

Goodluck Ebele Azikiwe Jonathan was born November 20, 1957, and served as Vice President of Nigeria, before he was elevated to President after the death of President Umaru Musa Yar'Adua. He previously served as Deputy Governor and Governor of Bayelsa State.

Mohammed Namadi Sambo was born on August 2, 1954, and served as Vice President of Nigeria 2010 – 2015, on the platform of Peoples Democratic Party. He also served as Governor of Kaduna State 2007 -2010.

David Alechenu Bonaventure Mark was born in April of 1948, and served as President of the senate 2007- 2015 on the platform of Peoples Democratic Party. He previously served as a military Governor and commissioner.

Theodore Ahamefule Orji was born in 1950, and served as Governor of Abia State 2007 – 2015, on the platform of Peoples Democratic Party. He was chief of staff to former Governor Orji Uzor Kalu.

Murtala Nyako was born August 27, 1943, and served as Governor of Adamawa State 2007- 2014, on the platform of Peoples Democratic Party. He was impeached and removed from office.

Godswill Obot Akpabio was born December 9, 1962, and served as Governor of Akwa Ibom State 2007 – 2015 on the platform of Peoples Democratic Party. He currently serves as minority leader in the senate.

Isa Yuguda was born June 15, 1956, and served as Governor of Bauchi State 2007 – 2011, on the platform of All Nigerian Peoples Party, but lost his reelection bid. He was previously a minister.

Henry Seriake Dickson was born January 28, 1966, and serves as Governor of Bayelsa State since February 20012, on the platform of Peoples Democratic Party. He was a member of the House of Representatives.

Gabriel Torwua Suswam was born November 15, 1964, and served as Governor of Benue State 2007 – 2015 on the platform of Peoples Democratic Party. He was unsuccessful as a candidate to the senate.

Liyel Imoke was born on July 10, 1961, and served as Governor of Cross River State 2007- 2015, on the platform of Peoples Democratic Party. He previously served as minister for mines and power, and education.

Ali Modu Sheriff was born in 1956, and served as Governor of Borno State 2003 – 2011, on the platform of All Nigerian Peoples Party. He previously served in the senate 1992- 93 and again 1999-2003, and was Chairman of Peoples Democratic Party. He is alleged to have funded the murderous Boko Haram sect.

Oserheimen Osunbor was born October 5, 1951, and served as Governor of Edo State 2007 – 2008, on the platform of Peoples Democratic Party. He previously served in the senate.

Emmanuel Eweta Uduaghan was born October 22, 154, and served as Governor of Delta State 2007 -2015, on the platform of Peoples Democratic Party. He previously served as commissioner for health and as secretary to the government.

Martin Elechi served as Governor of Ebonyi State 2007- 2015, on the platform of Peoples Democratic Party. He was a seasoned politician before becoming governor.

Adams Aliyu Oshiomhole was born on April 4, 1952, and serves as Governor of Edo State since 2008, on the platform of Action Congress of Nigeria. He was a former President of Nigeria Labour Congress.

Patrick Ibrahim Yakowa (December 1, 1948 – December 15, 2012) served as Governor of Kaduna State from May20, 2010, on the platform of Peoples Democratic Party until his death in a plane clash.

Olusegun Oni was born September 5, 1954, and served as Governor of Ekiti State May 2007 – October 2010, on the platform of Peoples Democratic Party. He is currently a member of All Progressives Congress.

Kashim Shettima was born September 2, 1966, and serving as Governor of Borno State since May 2011, on the platform of All Nigerian Peoples Party. He currently serves under All Progressives Congress.

Mukhtar Ramalan Yero was born May 1, 1968, and served as Governor of Kaduna State from December 2012 – May 2015, on the platform of Peoples Democratic Party. He previously served as Deputy Governor.

Koyade Fayemi was born on February 9, 1965, and served as Governor of Ekiti State from October 15, 2010 - October 16, 2014, on the platform of Action Congress of Nigeria. He is currently the minister for solid mineral development.

Sullivan Iheanacho Chime was born April 10, 1959, and served as Governor of Anambra State 2007 – 2015, on the platform of Peoples Democratic Party. He previously served as attorney general and commissioner for justice.

Ikedi Ohakim was born on August 4, 1957 and served as Governor of Imo State 2007 – 2011, on the platform of Progressive Peoples Alliance. He defected to Peoples Democratic Party and lost his reelection bid.

Ibrahim Hassan Dankwambo was born on April 4, 1962, and serves as Governor of Gombe State since May 2011, on the platform of Peoples Democratic Party.

**Sule Lamido** was born in 1948, and served as Governor of Jigawa State May 2007 – May 2015, on the platform of Peoples Democratic Party. He previously served as foreign minister.

Rochas Anayo Okorocha was born on September 22, 1962, and serves as Governor of Imo State since May 2011, on the platform of All Progressive Grand Alliance. He defected to All Progressives Congress and won reelection.

Ibrahim Shehu Shema was born on September 22, 1952, and served as Governor of Katsina State May 2007 – May 2015, on the platform of Peoples Democratic Party.

Babatunde Raji Fashola was born June 28, 1963, and served as Governor of Lagos State May 2007 – May 2015, on the platform of Action Congress of Nigeria. He currently serves as minister of power, works, and housing in Muhammadu Buhari administration.

Usman saidu Nasamu Dakingari was born September 13, 1959, and served as Governor of Kebbi State May 2007 – May 2015, on the platform of Peoples Democratic Party.

Ibrahim Idris was born in 1949, and served as Governor of Kogi State May 2003 – January 2012, on the platform of Peoples Democratic Party.

Mu'azu Babangida Aliyu was born on November 12, 1955, and serves as Governor of Niger State May 2007 – May 2015 on the platform of Peoples Democratic Party. He was a senior civil servant before entering politics.

Umaru Tanko Al-Makura was born in August 1952, and serves as Governor of Nasarawa State since May 2011, on the platform of Congress for Progressive Change. He was reelected in May 2015, on the platform of All Progressives Congress.

Abdulfatah Ahmed was born on December 29, 1959, and serves as Governor of Kwara State since May 2011, on the platform of Peoples Democratic Party. He currently serves on the platform of All Progressives Congress, and was commissioner for finance and economic development in the state.

Olusegun Mimiko was born October 3, 1954, and serves as Governor of Ondo State since February 2009, on the platform of Labour Party. He won reelection in October 2012 on the same platform before switching to Peoples Democratic Party.

Ibikunle Oyelaja Amosun was born on January 25, 1958, and serves as Governor of Ogun State since May 2011, on the platform of Action Congress of Nigeria. He now serves on the platform of All Progressives Congress, and previously served in the senate.

Rauf Aregbesola was born on May 25, 1957, and serves as Governor of Osun State since November 27, 2010, on the platform of Action Congress of Nigeria. He now serves on the platform of All Progressives Congress, and was Lagos State commissioner for works and infrastructure.

Isiaka Abiola Adeyemi Ajimobi was born on December 16, 1949, and serving as Governor of Oyo State since May 2011, on the platform of Action Congress of Nigeria and All Progressives Congress. He was previously a senator.

Jonah David Jang was born on March 13, 1944, and served as Governor of Plateau State May 2007 – May 2015, on the platform of Peoples Democratic Party. He was a military Governor in Benue and Gongola states.

Chibuike Rotimi Amaechi was born on May 27, 1965, and served as Governor of Rivers State October 2007 – May 2015 on the platform of Peoples Democratic Party. He later switched to All Progressives Congress and currently serves as minister of transport in Muhammadu Buhari administration.

Aliyu Magatakarda Wamakko was born on March 1, 1953, and served as Governor of Sokoto State from May 2007 – May 2015, on the platform of Peoples Democratic Party. He previously served as Deputy Governor.

Mahmud Aliyu Shinkafi served as governor of Zamfara State from May 2007 – May 2011, on the platform of All Nigerian Peoples Party. He changed parties and lost his reelection bid.

Danbaba Danfulani Suntai was born on June 30, 1961, and served as Governor of Taraba State from May 29, 2007 on the platform of Peoples Democratic Party, until he was paralyzed in a plane crash.

Ibrahim Geidam was born on September 15, 1956, and serving as Governor of Yobe State since January 27, 2009, on the platform of All Nigerian Peoples Party. He now serves under All Progressives Congress.

Abdul'aziz Yari Abubakar was born January 1st 1969, and serving as Governor of Zamfara State since May 29, 2011, on the platform of All Nigerian Peoples Party. He now serves under All Progressives Congress.

Muhammadu Buhari was born December 17, 1942, and serving as President of Nigeria since May 29, 2015. He previously served as military head of state from December 31, 1983 – August 27, 1985, and was Governor of North Eastern State, and commissioner for petroleum and natural resources.

Oluyemi Oluleke Osinbajo was born on March 8, 1957, and serving as Vice President of Nigeria since May 29, 2015. He was a professor of law at University of Lagos, and prior to that was Lagos State attorney general and commissioner for justice.

Bukola Saraki was born on December 19, 1962, and serving as President of the Nigeria senate since May 2015, on the platform of All Progressives Congress. He previously served as Governor of Kwara State.

Ike Ekweremadu was born on May 12, 1962, and serving as Deputy President of the senate since May 2015, on the platform of Peoples Democratic Party. He is serving his fourth term in the senate.

Okezie Victor Ikpeazu was born on October 18, 1964, and serving as Governor of Abia State since May 29, 2015, on the platform of Peoples Democratic Party.

Umaru Jibrilla Bindow is serving as Governor of Adamawa State since May 29, 2015, on the platform of All Progressives Congress. He was previously a senator.

Udom Gabriel Emmanuel was born on July 11, 1966, and serving as Governor of Akwa Ibom State since May 29, 2015, on the platform of Peoples Democratic Party.

William Obiano was born on August 8, 1955, and serving as Governor of Anambra State since March 17, 2014, on the platform of All Progressives Grand Alliance. He was previously a banker.

Mohammed Abdullahi Abubakar was born on December 11, 1956, and serving as Governor of Bauchi State since May 29, 2015, on the platform of All Progressives Congress.

Samuel Ortom was born on April 23, 1963, and serving as Governor of Benue State since May 29, 2015 on the platform of All Progressives Congress. He was previously a minister in Goodluck Jonathan administration.

Benedict Ayade was born March 2, 1969, and serving as Governor of Cross River State since May 29, 2015, on the platform of Peoples Democratic Party. He was previously a senator.

Arthur Ifeanyi Okowa was born on July 8, 1959, and serving as Governor of Delta State since May 29, 2015, on the platform of Peoples Democratic Party. He was previously a senator.

David Nweze Umahi was born on January 1st 1964, and serving as Governor of Ebonyi State since May 29, 2015, on the platform of Peoples Democratic Party. He was previously a Deputy Governor.

Lawrence Ifeanyi Ugwuanyi was born in March, 1964, and serving as Governor of Enugu State since May 29, 2015, on the platform of Peoples Democratic Party. He was previously a member of the House of Representatives.

Badaru Abubakar was born September 29, 1962, and serving as Governor of Jigawa State since May 29, 2015, on the platform of All Progressives Congress. He was a businessman prior to joining politics.

Nasir Ahmad El-Rufai was born on February 16, 1960, and serving as Governor of Kaduna State since May 29, 2015, on the platform of All Progressives Congress. He previously served as minister for the federal capital territory.

Abdullahi Umar Ganduje was born on December 25, 1949, and serving as Governor of Kano State since May 29, 2015, on the platform of All Progressives Congress. He was previously a Deputy Governor.

Aminu Bello Masari was born on May 29, 1950, and serving as Governor of Katsina State since May 29, 2015, on the platform of All Progressives Congress. He previously served as speaker of the House of Representatives.

Abubakar Atiku Bagudu was born December 26, 196, and serving as Governor of Kebbi State since May 29, 2015, on the platform of All Progressives Congress. He was previously a senator.

Yahaya Bello was born on June 18, 1975, and serving as Governor of Kogi State since May 29, 2015, on the platform of All Progressives Congress. He was a businessman prior to running for elective office.

Akinwunmi Ambode was born on June 14, 1963, and serving as Governor of Lagos State since May 29, 2015, on the platform of All Progressives Congress. He previously served as accountant general of Lagos State.

Abubakar Sani Bello was born on December 17, 1967, and serving as Governor of Niger State since May 29, 2015, on the platform of All Progressives Congress. He was a businessman prior to seeking elective office.

Simon Bako Lalong was born on May 5, 1963, and serving as Governor of Plateau State since May 29, 2015, on the platform of All Progressives Congress. He previously served as speaker of the state assembly.

Ezenwo Nyesom Wike was born on December 13, 1967, and serving as Governor of Rivers State since May 29, 2015, on the platform of Peoples Democratic Party. He was previously minister of state for education.

Aminu Waziri Tambuwal was born on July 10, 1966, and serving as Governor of Sokoto State since May 29, 2015, on the platform of All Progressives Congress. He was previously speaker of the House of Representatives.

Darius Dickson Ishaku was born on July 30, 1954, and serving as Governor of Taraba State since May29, 2015, on the platform of Peoples Democratic Party. He was a businessman prior to joining politics.

Fourth republic political leaders introduced unusual measure of ethnic sentiments into politics and gave leaders of sectional groups a great opening in national dialogue.

References

Konde, Emmanuel, May 29, 2009. "How the Igbo came to Dominate Victoria", Up station mountain club
Mbile, N.N, July 26, 2011, Cameroon Political History: Memories of an Authentic Eye Witness, Langaa RPCIG.
The Christian walk, June 3, 2015 "Why President Jonathan lost the 2015 presidential election and things to come under President Muhammadu Buhari (2015 - 2019) part one. The Nigerian voice

This book was written in conjunction with Mbonu Ojike Institute for Public Policy Research.

www.ingramcontent.com/pod-product-compliance
Lightning Source LLC
Chambersburg PA
CBHW030526290526
45786CB00004B/1633